Victoria

Wedding Cakes

Victoria

Wedding Cakes

Text by Kathleen Hackett

Hearst Books
A Division of
Sterling Publishing Co., Inc.
New York

Book design by
Alexander Isley Inc.

Text by Kathleen Hackett

Library of Congress Cataloging-in-Publication Data

Hackett, Kathleen.
   Wedding cakes / by Kathleen Hackett.
      p. cm.
Includes index.
   ISBN 1-58816-092-0
   1. Wedding cakes. 2. Cake decorating. I. Title.
TX771.H22 2003
641.8'653--dc21   2003001803
10 9 8 7 6 5 4 3 2 1

Published by Hearst Books
A Division of Sterling Publishing Co., Inc.
387 Park Avenue South, New York, NY 10016

Hearst Books is proud to continue the superb style, quality, and tradition of Victoria magazine with every book we publish. On our beautifully illustrated pages you will always find inspiration and ideas about the subjects you love.

Victoria is a trademark owned by Hearst Magazines Property, Inc., in USA, and Hearst Communications, Inc., in Canada. Hearst Books is a trademark owned by Hearst Communications, Inc.

Distributed in Canada by Sterling Publishing
c/o Canadian Manda Group, One Atlantic Avenue, Suite 105
Toronto, Ontario, Canada M6K 3E7

Distributed in Australia by Capricorn Link (Australia) Pty. Ltd.
P.O. Box 704, Windsor, NSW 2756 Australia

Manufactured in China

ISBN 1 58816-092-0

Page 2: A charming, single-tiered cake covered in drifts of coconut needs only a homespun tablecloth and a simple glass cake stand to look stylish.

In all of the wedding cake,
hope is the sweetest of plums.

—Douglas Jerrold

Contents

Introduction

Wedding cakes are as magical as romance and as varied as brides and grooms. Today the classic tiered white wedding cake is only one of the many styles a couple can choose from. The sweetest symbol of a couple's new life together, a wedding cake can be a towering stack of tiers separated by columns and bursting with flowers, a charming layer cake swathed in swirls of seven-minute frosting, an architectural wonder with crisp edges covered in fondant or even a tower of cupcakes. The cake can also be more personal. There are hundreds of ways to tastefully incorporate favorite flowers, a beloved lace pattern, and the details of a wedding dress onto a wedding cake.

Victoria *Wedding Cakes* is designed to inspire you to consider the unlimited possibilities for your wedding cake, both on the outside and inside. There is almost nothing a talented baker can't do, as you will see on the pages that follow. If the fresh flowers you love are out of season, have them rendered in butter cream instead. If your favorite color is woven throughout your ceremony and reception, then ask your baker if a tinted cake would be possible. If you and your groom are nature lovers, discuss the possibilities for conveying the mountains or woodlands or seashore that you love on your cake. Carrot, lemon, chocolate or spice, whatever flavor you fancy can surely become part of your wedding cake choice. Drape the layers in royal icing, butter cream, fondant, Swiss meringue, chocolate or *seven-minute* frosting, whichever is your favorite.

Whether you are celebrating in front of the fire in your living room or in the grand ballroom of a hotel, you will find these pages brimming with ideas and essential information for creating the cake of your dreams.

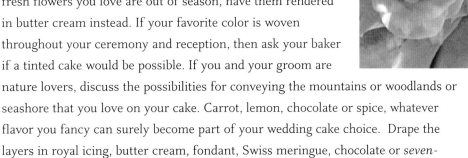

Opposite: *A classic white cake covered in fondant and draped with pearls of royal icing is always elegant. The tightly bound topper of pink roses adds a romantic blush of color.*

CHAPTER I

The Dream

Something old, something new, something borrowed, something blue . . . For generations, tradition has allowed the bride to choose her wedding dress as well as mementos and keepsakes to create her own very personal vision of something old, new, borrowed, and blue. However, when it came to the wedding cake there was no latitude for choice. Traditionally, it had to be a three-tiered white-frosted cake with a plastic or porcelain bride and groom perched on top.

Times have changed. Modern wedding cakes are far more reflective of a couple's shared personal style. In fact, there are probably as many different weddings cakes as there are brides and grooms. For many couples, the wedding cake makes a vivid style statement—as important as the wedding dress and the venue they choose to marry in. If you think back to the last three or four weddings you attended, chances are that each cake was vastly different from the other—and one was probably saturated in color! As a bride-to-be you will find hundreds of wedding cake styles, colors, and flavors to choose from, and the traditional white tiered cake is just one of them.

The "something blue" at a wedding today could well be the cake.

Your wedding reception is likely to be the most elaborate party you will ever give and your wedding cake the most memorable dessert you will ever serve. Displayed at the reception with the same reverence as a beloved work of art, your wedding cake should be given as much consideration as every other major decision you make about your big day. How your cake looks is of utmost importance, but how it tastes is an equally important reflection of your personal style and unique sensibility.

Whether your taste runs toward the traditional or the modern, the style of your wedding cake is only as limited as your imagination and the mood you want to create at your big party. If you want a teetering tower of layer cakes bursting with gum-paste flowers on every surface, tell your cake designer and discuss how to make your dream a reality. If you've always envisioned a three-tiered, white-frosted cake with a traditional topper, then that is what you should have. But if a rich chocolate layer cake with chocolate butter-cream frosting bedecked in deep red roses reflects your passion, then don't hesitate to put that on display for all your guests to marvel at.

Page 10: A swath of roses skims across a three-tiered white cake, dressing it up for the occasion. An experienced baker can create almost any flower desired in frosting.

Right: Your wedding cake can be anything you want it to be, so long as it reflects your personal style. For one couple with a shared passion for flower gardening, a tower of cupcakes in full bloom struck the perfect note at their casual outdoor reception.

Opposite: Two dozen yellow rosebuds carpet the top of this festive, two-tiered cake, perfectly suited for a small restaurant wedding. Lush cornflower satin ribbon delineates the tiers and adds a colorful note to what began as a traditional white cake.

There are a few decisions, however, that are best made before you choose what kind of wedding cake you will have. Determine the date, location, and number of guests attending your wedding before you begin to fantasize about the cake of your dreams. Once you have made these decisions, your wedding will begin to have a specific feeling, mood, or theme, which should be echoed in the style of your cake. The season of your wedding, the size of the cake needed, and the accessibility of the wedding site can also influence your choice of flavors, ingredients, and decoration. Once you have confirmed the logistical details, you can begin to talk to a baker and seek out inspiration for a cake that is uniquely yours.

Right and opposite: Your cake doesn't have to be formal. A casual summer wedding at the beach inspired this sweet seashell confection.

Inspiration is All Around You

There are hundreds of places to seek inspiration for your wedding cake style, many of them closer than you might think. Of course, magazines and books are sure to spark your creativity, but to achieve a truly individual—and memorable—sweet ending to your blissful day, just look around you.

Your dress is an excellent, and many bakers will tell you, the only source of inspiration needed to make a glorious wedding cake. Most cake bakers will ask you to bring your dress to them so that they can see the color, texture, and stylistic details up close. The color can easily be translated to the icing if you're after an elegant, monochromatic theme. What's more, buttons, bows, ruffles, and pleats can all be re-created on a cake to mimic the style of your dress. If your dress is covered in passementerie, that too can be rendered on the tiers of the cake in butter-cream or gum-paste scrolls.

In addition, it helps before visiting your baker to put together a mini scrapbook of words, pictures, swatches, and any other items that will help convey your vision for your wedding cake.

Opposite: A four-tiered, all white cake can be both grand and understated at the same time. This confection is simply adorned with only slender swags looping along each tier, a bouquet of gum-paste roses on top, and a ring of gardenias for table decoration.

Left, top: A crown of fresh garden roses in varying shades of pink rings a single tier, the perfect cake for a small, elegant summer reception at home.

Left, bottom: Inspired by a set of beloved family china passed from one generation to the next, one bride honored tradition by having the nostalgic pattern translated onto her cake.

Include that piece of lace you have been saving just because you love it. And don't hesitate to add the paint chip with the color you painted your favorite room. And what about a swatch of that dotted Swiss dress your mother surprised you with on your tenth birthday?

Most patterns, colors, and textures can be re-created on your cake by an expert cake baker. Could the sweet floral pattern on the cherished handkerchief from your grandmother provide the decoration inspiration for a beautiful and poignant cake?

The **seasons** are also wonderful sources of **inspiration,** particularly if you are marrying on or near a **holiday.**

Can you picture the family china that has been passed on to you translated into beautifully colored swirls of frosting?

Consider the location of your wedding as a source of inspiration, too. A woodland setting may suggest a cake draped in elegant butter-cream greenery depicting ferns or hostas. If your party is under a tent in an open field of wildflowers, by all means, consider incorporating them into your cake. If you are having an elaborate celebration in a fancy hotel ballroom, look closely at the décor and architecture of the room; there may be shapes and colors that are beautifully suited to the structure and decoration of your cake.

The seasons are also wonderful sources of inspiration, particularly if you are marrying on or near a holiday. Are you planning a spring wedding in Vermont? What could be more charming and delicious than a maple sugar layer cake to evoke the state's most delicious delicacy? Are you getting married in the Pacific Northwest this summer, when huckleberries are at their peak? Nothing makes a cake look more enticing than fresh, abundant regional fruit. A Christmas wedding cake can be as ethereal as a snowy coconut layer cake or as over-the-top as a lavishly decorated tree-shaped cake iced in chocolate and sprinkled with powdered sugar to imitate fallen snow.

Opposite: A wedding cake can be a poignant reference to your ancestry. This traditional Scandinavian wedding cake—a towering pyramid of marzipan rings, each drizzled with white royal icing—is as breathtaking as any wedding cake can be.

If your family history and traditions have played a strong role in your life, perhaps you should look to your heritage for clues to creating a memorable wedding cake. If you hail from a strong French lineage—or maybe you first vacationed with your betrothed in Paris—you may consider forgoing a traditional layer cake and do as the French do: Celebrate the occasion with a **croquembouche**, an elaborate dessert made with caramel-coated custard-filled cream puffs stacked into a tall pyramid and draped in spun sugar. A bride of Scandinavian descent might choose the Danish marzipan ring cake, the customary wedding cake in Denmark. A masterpiece of almonds, pastillage, and marzipan, this cake is filled with fresh fruit, candy, and almond cakes.

If you love the idea of acknowledging your heritage but don't care for the wedding cakes found in your ancestral country, consider creating a cake from other traditional sweets and confections. The wonderful and colorful variety of Italian cookies available in good Italian bakeries make clever and delicious

"cakes" when artfully stacked in tiers. And why not honor your Mexican bloodlines by sculpting a pyramid of Mexican wedding cakes, the powdered sugar-covered shortbread cookies so popular during the holidays. Don't hesitate to mention your favorite sweet or dessert to your baker, no matter how irrelevant it may seem. It may spark an idea that you thought impossible to create.

Ideas can come from seemingly unlikely places; even scenes from still-life paintings are rich resources, if not for the specific cake and its decorations then certainly for the mood they can inspire you to create. Chardin, Vermeer, Manet, Monet, Degas, Van Gogh, and more contemporary artists such as Wayne Thiebaud render shapes, colors, and emotions that may be exactly what you want to convey with your cake. Chardin's "The Buffet" for example, features a towering pyramid of fresh fruit made from an assemblage of several compotes arranged at varying heights—a concept you may be able to re-create with an assemblage of cakes. You could also look at paintings and ceramics in your local museums or in art books at your local library or bookstore.

Movies, too, can spark moods and visual ideas that can be extended to your wedding cake. The French movie **Chocolat** may inspire an all-chocolate extravaganza, while **Babette's Feast** could convince you that a buffet reception with a fabulous cake as the centerpiece suits your style perfectly. Pick up videos and look at **The Wedding Banquet, Like Water for Chocolate, Eat Drink Man Woman,** and **Chef in Love**. All movies centered on food and feasting, they are sure to awaken your creativity,

And don't feel you have to arrive at your baker's with dozens of ideas. If you are the kind of bride who knows exactly what you want, the items in your scrapbook may be limited to one or two entries. If you can't imagine a cake without your favorite flower, berry, or tree incorporated into the cake, then that's all you need to show your baker.

The shape of the modern three-tiered iced cake is believed to have been inspired by the spire of Saint Bride's Church in the City of London.

Opposite: A classic white cake can be used as a canvas for all manner of decoration. A cornucopia of vibrant roses tumbling down the tiers gives this otherwise quiet white confection flamboyance and style.

CHAPTER 2

Sweet Possibilities

Classic White Cakes

It is the color of purity and a symbol of innocence. When white is baked into the layers of a wedding cake and spun into icing that graces each tier in loopy swirls, exacting patterns, or in a smooth gleaming coat, only the bride herself can compare to its breathtaking beauty. White weddings are as timeless as matrimony itself, and a classic white wedding cake will only emphasize a couple's reverence for the rituals of love and marriage.

White wedding cakes first appeared in Victorian times, when only affluent families were able to obtain the finest refined sugars for making icing. In those days, the more refined and expensive the sugar, the whiter the cake. No longer an indication of affluence, a classic white wedding cake remains among the most popular with bridal couples, both for celebrating the strong traditions associated with a wedding day as well as for evoking endless visions of individual style.

Time was when all white wedding cakes looked and tasted essentially the same. Traditionally, three tiers were separated by columns and draped with white royal icing. Today, a white wedding cake can take on many shapes, styles, and even

flavors, depending on the personal style of the bridal couple. Cakes can range in presentation from fanciful and playful to stately and majestic, and in flavors as delicate as orange blossom or vanilla bean to more assertive versions such as toasted almond or white chocolate.

The only rules a couple need follow are the obvious: To qualify as classic a white wedding cake must be white inside and out and arranged in tiers, on columns or stacked. The shape may be square, round, oval, hexagonal, or petal. In addition to the traditional royal icing, the tiers can be frosted in fondant, Swiss meringue butter cream, white chocolate ganache, and seven-minute frosting.

Page 22: Something blue? A classic white cake swathed in butter cream and bursting with roses is beautifully embellished with an eggshell-blue ribbon.

Opposite: The smooth tiers of a white wedding cake are set on dowels to give this cake height. Tiny rosebuds tightly tucked in between provide both beautiful and textural layers to the cake and hide the framework that holds it steady. The piped butter-cream ruffles make the confection flow seamlessly from cake layer to rosebuds.

This page: The classic five-tiered white cake is always visually stunning. The flowers chosen for your bouquet can also provide the perfect finishing touch for your cake.

Page 26: Single strands of gleaming silver dragées are exquisite when used sparingly, as they are in this refined white fondant-covered cake. Gum-paste roses spill modestly across the tiers without compromising its manicured look, while a silk bow topper adds a whimsical air.

All are beautiful and delicious, but each one has special attributes, which may make it more or less ideal for the effect you want to create. Royal icing was at one time the only frosting considered appropriate for white wedding cakes. Today it is used to evoke even more elaborate and decorative effect than in Victorian times. It is a wonderful medium for creating piped decorations, which can be fashioned into bows and swags to swing around a cake, or into decorative borders to give the cake a finished look. It is also the perfect medium for gluing decorations to the cake.

Swiss meringue butter cream can be applied in broad strokes for an informal, whimsical look, or it can be piped through all manner of tips to create lush, yet precise, traditional patterns such as wickerwork and ruffles or designs that echo the details of the bride's white dress. In fact, Swiss meringue butter cream is so versatile that it can be used to render elements of the wedding setting right onto the cake. For example, if your celebration is in a clapboard cottage by the sea, the clapboard pattern can be piped right onto the cake. If you have your heart set

Page 27: Sugar dough ribbons and flowers come to life when arranged as if tumbling down the smooth tiers of a classic white wedding cake.

Right, top: Nature seems to produce flowers in every color imaginable—even those on your favorite china pattern. Study the colors you want to duplicate and then determine which flowers best mimic them. Choose those that are appropriately sized for your cake, and be sure that they will stay fresh through the reception.

Right, bottom: If special occasions always mean pulling out the family china, then what better celebration than a wedding—and more delicious medium than a wedding cake—to recall the pattern? Cascades of fresh flowers and bands of grosgrain ribbon adorn this traditional white cake, bringing a treasured china pattern to life.

SWEET POSSIBILITIES

on a pure white cake, however, keep in mind that butter cream—made with butter—is actually the color of ivory.

If you're after a formal, tailored look, consider fondant, a pliable sugar dough that can be rolled out and draped onto the tiers of a cake for a satiny smooth finish. Fondant not only provides an incomparably smooth surface on which to arrange cake decorations but can be used as a canvas for making impressions, from quilted patterns made with a dressmaker's wheel to repeated borders made by pressing a piping tip into the fondant itself.

A classic white wedding cake is best compared to the little black dress: It is always fitting, unerringly timeless, and always looks good. You can dress it up or down (butter cream, royal icing, or fondant?), depending on the mood and tone you want to set. White embellishments—fresh, crystallized, or gum-paste flowers; royal icing or gum-paste ruffles, lace, swirls, swags, buttons, bows, petals, leaves, shells, dots, and zigzags—can bedeck the tiers. And with the variety of flavorings and fillings available now, it is sure to taste fabulous.

Left, top: *Expert cake artists can translate almost any dream of a cake into a reality. For one bride, an elaborately decorated porcelain box just had to inform her wedding cake design. Three tiers are stacked one atop the other, covered in tinted fondant, and bedecked with royal icing. A fourth tier is an exact replica of the box and the perfect place to tuck a tiny posy of fresh flowers.*

Left, bottom: *Bands of gold royal icing are remarkable imitations of the hinged and clasped box.*

Colorful Cakes

A wedding cake drenched in color is always a showstopper, particularly if it aptly reflects the personalities and styles of the bride and groom. For some couples, a colorful cake is deeply meaningful, in some cases a tribute to a beloved family member or heirloom. Great-grandmother's patterned handkerchief, the flamboyant family china, the 1940s wallpaper that still hangs in the summer cottage, mother's Fabergé jewel box—even the antique fabric from grandfather's favorite chair—can all be rendered in icing and decorations on your cake.

Because colorful cakes can be so magnificent, they are becoming more popular. Artist Wendy Kromer's Wedgwood cake echoes the patterns of the classic china. It is a masterpiece of blue-tinted fondant tiers decorated with creamy white designs and is a frequent choice with the clients of her wedding cake "boutique." A close second in popularity among her customers is her primrose cake, in which vividly colored flowers come to life against soft-toned icing to mimic the Tuscan Majolica earthenware that inspired it.

Whether you envision your wedding cake awash in color in both the icing and decorations, or displaying eye-popping decorations fixed against a classic white background, there are many ways to incorporate color into your wedding cake. If it is

Above: Blown sugar pearls of ivory and gold bob and weave along the tiers of a whimsical "painted" cake that is anything but conventional. A passion for impressionist art might inspire a cake such as this.

difficult to choose a single color, consider covering the layers in different tones of one hue or alternating two shades, such as pink and lavender. If a classic white cake **and** color are appealing, satisfy both desires by frosting the tiers in colored ribbons of marzipan or butter cream.

Of course, your cake can be any color you like, but consult your cake baker before you set your heart on a particular shade. While most cake professionals can achieve the impossible, experience has taught them that some icing and decoration materials take better to certain colors than others. If you want your cake to look as mouthwatering as it is awe-inspiring you may have to make minor adjustments to match both cake and frosting to your chosen color.

You might also take your color cues from the colors and flavors of the season. A spring wedding might inspire a cake mirroring the various shades of young spring greenery. An autumn wedding, on the other hand, lends itself beautifully to a cake covered in golden,

Page 31: The open weave of this royal iced cake creates just enough space to add tiny lavender designs, giving an overall impression that the cake is not white. A generous bundle of deeper-purple sweet peas reinforces the "color" of this otherwise simple white confection. All the while featherweight butterflies made from royal icing flutter along the tiers.

Right: The cake stand can also add to the visual impact of a wedding cake. Here color is used only sparingly on the cake itself. Instead, it is concentrated in the cake stand, with small hints of hue appearing in fine bands and flowers on the cake's tiers.

SWEET POSSIBILITIES

red, orange, and yellow leaves rendered in marzipan, butter cream, or royal icing. Seasonal flavors can also dictate the colors of a cake. A winter wedding cake might feature the fruit colors of the season—citrus yellows, oranges, greens, and reds—or the warmer, richer tones of chocolate and nuts. A couple getting married on the seashore need only take a walk on the beach to find breezy color inspiration. The variously shaded blues and greens of sea glass; the corals, pinks, violets, and silvers of seashells; and the sky, water, sand, and grasses can all be echoed sweetly on a summer wedding cake.

The most obvious place to look for color inspiration is the flowers you will carry, the decorations you've chosen for the ceremony and the reception, and the colors you've chosen for the wedding party. Wherever you find the colors that best reflect your style, arrive at your meeting with your cake designer with the colorful swatches and objects that you hope to translate onto your cake. No amount of verbal description can replace seeing the real thing.

THEIR PIECE OF CAKE

No matter where couples live, they have two requirements when it comes to choosing a wedding cake: It must taste delicious and look beautiful, whether simple and elegant, or ornate and stately. Still, there are some regional preferences.

New York City—Square, stacked cakes with neoclassical designs are very popular.

New England—Flavor rules: Chocolate cake with chocolate ganache filling and icing is a favorite; so are lemon pound cake with raspberry filling and butter-cream frosting, carrot cake with butter-cream filling and frosting; chocolate cake with chocolate mousse filling.

Chicago/Midwest—Pillars are still favored here, and more and more couples are requesting square cakes. As for flavor, almond cake with custard filling and butter-cream frosting is a top choice.

Dallas, Texas—The traditional tiered white cake with white filling and either white chocolate ganache or fondant frosting is the top pick. It is most often decorated with simple, elegant pastillage flowers.

Floral Cakes

Like love and marriage, flowers and wedding cakes are made for each other. And for every couple choosing a wedding cake, there is a sweet combination that is perfectly suited to them. Flowers can dance delicately around each tier, as if casually scattered like wildflowers, or they can spill from tier to tier in tight bunches, spiraling grandly from top to bottom. They can cover every surface of a cake for a painterly look or bloom here and there on a smooth backdrop for a more graphic presentation. For the minimalist couple, flowers can show up in just one place, in a smartly arranged bouquet on top of the cake. Flowers can bring your personal style to life, whether you want to present your sweet and delicate side or that gregarious and eccentric streak. Perhaps the least contrived of all cake decorations, fresh flowers are an incomparable choice if your tastes run toward the fresh and natural.

Just as the bridal bouquet and any floral decorations are chosen with the season, availability, and viability in mind, so too should flowers be selected. Chances are, the flowers you choose for the other elements of your wedding will be incorporated into

Opposite: An array of pastel blooms is all the decoration this simple white cake needs to look lovely. But make sure any flowers you choose are sturdy enough to stay fresh throughout the reception.

Page 36: Roses and primroses seem to grow naturally from the base tiers of this charming cake. Two hexagonal tiers separated by a perfectly round one give the flowers several varied surfaces upon which to bloom.

FRESH FLOWERS FOR YOUR CAKE—WHICH ONES WORK BEST

Once you've chosen the fresh flowers to adorn your cake—and determined that they are safe—you will want to be confident that they will thrive throughout the wedding reception until the cake is cut. Experienced cake designers will have expert suggestions on which flowers hold up well in specific weather conditions and for the duration of the wedding celebration. New England wedding cake baker Christine Deonis prefers working with "cluster" flowers, including delphiniums, lilacs, hydrangea, stock, or larkspur because they can be snipped off individually and scattered onto the cake. Unfussy flowers, such as orchids, calla lilies, tulips, gardenias, and daisies also work well. Edible flowers are always a charming adornment, and there are many to choose from that will work beautifully, including violets, pansies, roses, chrysanthemums, Johnny jump-ups, lilacs, and petunias.

your cake. Be sure that your florist and wedding cake designer are informed of your desires. Who is responsible for the flowers on the cake, the florist or the cake designer? Be sure to coordinate their efforts.

While the possibilities for fresh-flower choices seem infinite, there are some limitations when it comes to those that grace your wedding cake. Flowers essentially fall into three categories: edible, which means you can eat them safely; nontoxic, flowers that are safe to use for decoration but must be removed before the cake is served; and toxic, which should never come into contact with a wedding cake. If you have your heart set on beautiful yet toxic daffodils, wisteria, sweet peas, or irises, make sure you've chosen a baker who can render them in icing. Your florist and cake designer will be able to tell you which flowers are appropriate. If a generous friend or amateur cake baker is making the cake and wants to use fresh flowers, be sure to check their safety with a professional. All fresh flowers used for decorating a cake, whether edible or nontoxic, should be grown pesticide-free (see box).

While fresh flowers are the easiest and least expensive way to achieve a beautiful cake, the seasonal and safety limitations are of no consequence if the blossoms are made from edible

Left and below: Nature lovers never want to be far from it and why should they? Buttercream bees and butterflies flit about the tiers of this colorful cake, their destination seeming to be the spray of silk flowers that adorns the top.

CAKE WISE

"If I am working with fresh flowers, I prefer to work with rolled fondant. It is easier to remove the flowers from the cake before serving it. I also prefer to place a precut piece of clear plastic or cellophane on the top of the tier where the flowers may touch the cake. You don't see the plastic and the flowers won't be in direct contact with the icing. Always notify whoever will be cutting the cake to remove ALL flowers unless they are edible."—Wendy Kromer, boutique wedding cake designer, New York City

ingredients. Cover an entire cake with lilies of the valley in piped butter cream, or replicate a field of black-eyed Susans in gum paste. If your favorite roses are difficult

to come by, ask your cake designer to craft them from sugar. Many cake designers make beautiful crystallized versions of flowers, too.

Cakes Inspired by Nature

Did you meet while hiking the Appalachian Trail? Or taking a canoeing class? Is your cabin in the woods your favorite getaway? Does a field of wildflowers remind you of your first date? Did he propose on a walk through the woods? More than ever before, couples are requesting cakes that serve as symbols of a memorable moment, place, or experience in their relationship. Cakes covered with butter-cream ferns, marzipan wild strawberries, Swiss meringue mushrooms, and gum-paste pinecones are as breathtaking as any, especially when they are tied to a romantic or poignant personal memory.

Cake designer Ron Ben-Israel once had a client request a cake dancing with buzzing marzipan bees on each tier. The bees were symbolic of the groom's commendable attempts to propose. In his first effort, he was down on his knee when a bee stung him, sending him to the hospital. In a repeat effort—this time indoors in the winter—another bee found him and stung him again. He succeeded on his third attempt. The tongue-in-cheek—and charming—reference to his perseverance, portrayed by the decorative bees on the wedding cake, forever etched in the couple's memories the moment of proposal.

Informal, Elegant Cakes

If you want your wedding day to exude a casual air, carry the mood right through to your cake. **Informal** does not mean "ordinary," and an unfussy cake is anything but when it is presented with elegance. Thoughtfully restraining the scale, size, and decorations on a wedding cake can create as much impact as a teetering tower of bedecked tiers. A simple cake can sport jaunty polka dots rendered in royal icing, as

Above: *Playful polka dots are piped in graphic columns and rows on this sweet cake, perfectly suited to an atmosphere that is both lighthearted and elegant.*

long as the accompanying decorations are scaled accordingly. Loopy swirls of seven-minute frosting are exquisite when they cover a small cake adorned only with shards of pure white coconut. A single-tiered, monochromatic cake decorated with a repeated piped pattern and set on a classic cake stand is handsome enough to star at a wedding luncheon or a small evening wedding.

   If you want to create an informal mood, and even a low-tiered layer cake still seems too imposing, consider a sheet cake. Covered in fondant, a square sheet cake is as intriguing as grandmother's jewel box. And decorated with fresh or gum-paste flowers, it is perfect for a wedding tea or luncheon. Or you can create a casual cake composed of several tiers, as long as it is covered with broad strokes of icing or with a sleek coat of fondant and ganache and sparingly decorated.

   One of the most popular ways to maintain an air of informality and still incorporate tiers is by arranging fancifully decorated cupcakes onto graduated sizes of cake stands, stacked to mimic the shape of a wedding cake. This playful choice allows guests several different flavors of cupcakes to choose from. Another plus, wedding cupcakes makes serving a breeze as there is no cake to cut—guests simply help themselves.

Opposite: Several small cakes have big impact when expertly decorated and presented. Variously shaped square and tall tiers plus a flamboyant topper give these cakes a personality all their own.

Above: A wedding tea calls for a delicate cake served on fine china. A square jewel-box of a confection, delicately decorated, is the perfect way to celebrate a simple ceremony at home.

CHAPTER 3

The Right Baker

Finding the right person to bake your wedding cake is as important as landing on a pair of wedding shoes that you can dance in all night. You need to find a good fit if you want to leave your wedding reception smiling. The best place to start is by asking friends whose wedding cakes you've remembered, both before and after they were cut. Most professional pastry chefs will leave their business cards with the reception staff or the bride; it is perfectly appropriate to ask for one if you like what you've seen and tasted.

Word of mouth can often turn up the best cake bakers. Perhaps your friend's friend works in the food business and can give you a list of proven bakers and pastry chefs, or your colleague's husband manages a banquet hall where hundreds of weddings are held each year. If a hotel or country club will be both hosting and catering the event, the staff wedding manager may strongly urge—or even require—that you use the in-house baker or one affiliated. The local telephone directory, bridal shops, bridal shows, and the Internet are all excellent places to begin your search.

A wedding planner, should you choose to work with one, can usually recommend a preferred baker or two. So, too, can most independent caterers or florists you interview. Be sure to see that person's portfolio and have a cake tasting before agreeing to use him or her. If you choose a different baker, inquire as to whether the venue adds an additional fee for cutting the cake. This is sometimes negotiable. Don't overlook your neighborhood bakery, even though they don't display wedding cakes in their window. They may make simple wedding cakes that are perfectly suited to your style.

You might even discover a gifted "cottage" baker with a passion for perfection, someone with experience who handles just a few special orders from home and does them beautifully. If your friend Annie or an enthusiastic relative who "loves making cakes" volunteers to make your wedding cake, a word of caution: It's not that a home-baked cake can't be delicious and pretty. But professional bakers have ovens, storage, and packing equipment as well as delivery and setup arrangements that help guarantee your cake arrives intact no matter the weather and survives intact to the grand moment of its cutting.

Regardless of the resources you use, make sure that you make appointments to meet the bakers three to six months in advance, especially if you plan to use a

popular cake designer, and if the person is a real star, a year ahead is occasionally required.

Since the early 1980s, when splendid wedding cakes by star bakers such as Sylvia Weinstock, Gail Watson, and Ron Ben-Israel became the breathtaking centerpieces of notable celebrations, more and more bakers throughout the country have studied and mastered the techniques of artistic decoration. Nowadays, you're far more likely to find such a person nearby than when your mom got married. Some skilled decorators offer just a few variations of flavors and fillings. But increasingly, brides are requesting, and getting, a cake that embodies the mouthwatering versatility of a true pâtissier.

Taste Before You Order

Some pastry chefs charge for consultations, while others factor it into the per/slice cost of the finished wedding cake. Ask what the policy is before you make the appointment and inquire, too, whether there will be samples to taste and pictures of previous work. If the baker hesitates to provide either of these, reconsider your choice. Though bakers with a bridal specialty can show you portfolios of their previous

Opposite: A lush buttercream ruffle rings the top of a single-tiered cake set on a rimmed glass cake stand. Stephanotis, a classic wedding flower, and delicate purple blooms are just the right scale for this petite yet shapely cake.

Left: Why not add a touch of whimsy to your wedding? If a tree of chocolate gum-paste leaves is what you desire, then your cake baker can surely make it. On this fun-loving cake, individually wired leaves are tucked into the tree's "trunk" and set off-center on the top.

creations, and many today have websites as well, there's no substitute for a visit, a tasting, and a personal consultation. This is the time to discuss your ideas, consider new ones, and get an idea of the costs involved.

Remember that the more renowned the baker, the busier and the farther ahead you may need to lock in your dates. Have you finally landed on a date when your favorite inn on the lake is available? Alas, that doesn't mean the baker is also free that day. The busy season for weddings now stretches well beyond June and includes major holidays. In fact, early autumn, with its dazzling weather, is almost as popular a time for vows as early summer. So if you are enthusiastic about the baker, book your date. Most wedding cake designers prefer to meet couples after they have made most of the major wedding day decisions: date, time of day, venue, basic style. If all the lovely details—aside from the date—have not yet come together, you and the baker can always fine-tune the cake design later.

There are several questions, both practical and fanciful, that your baker will ask in order to help you create the cake of your wedding-day dreams. On the practical side, he or she will need to know such basic information as wedding date, place (indoors

Right: A multitiered "cake" can also be created in cupcakes. In this tower, 50 cupcakes are arranged in graduated tiers with a two-layer cake on top. Sunflowers and hydrangeas are rendered in butter cream, dressing the crest of each cupcake as well as the top tier.

Opposite: The simplest decorations can be the most showstopping. A simple, sleekly iced white cake needs only a few tiny, colorful flowers to make an impact.

or out, accompanied by a photo), time, number of guests, and style of reception (tea, luncheon, sit-down dinner, buffet, formal, informal). Your budget is essential.

For the more creative element of the conversation, most bakers want to get a sense of a bridal couple's personality, which makes it very important that all meet in person before any decisions are made. In addition to the basic information detailed above, be prepared to offer descriptions of the type of decorations (flowers, fabrics, colors, favors) planned for the reception, details and style of the bridal and bridal-party dresses, headpieces and any other flourish that is part of the bridal ensemble (including shoes!), if and what family wedding traditions will be part of the celebration, and whether there is anything about your relationship that may possibly be used in the design of the cake. Some couples prefer to reference the place where the proposal was made, while others are eager to display their profession (usually if it's shared) or a passion for a specific animal, sport, or hobby in the design of the cake. The possibilities are limitless.

Tiered, Layered, or Sheet—Which Style Suits Yours?

A wedding cake can be anything you want it to be—contemporary, dramatic, ornate, regal, simple, or homespun. Perhaps you've long dreamed of an all-white wedding, from your dress and flowers to the traditional, dreamy, three-tiered wedding cake, filled with butter cream and covered in white icing. Now that the day is almost here, the traditional tiered cake seems a bit too ordinary, or perhaps it doesn't fit with the casual mood you want to create.

The style of your wedding will also influence the shape and, more importantly, the structure of your cake. For an at-home luncheon for forty, an elaborate tiered cake is hardly necessary or appropriate, whereas an extravagant ballroom wedding lends itself beautifully to a towering cake. A round, tiered cake is tradition bound while a square stacked cake reflects a more contemporary style. A heart shape—

Opposite: Be sure to discuss the cake stand with your cake designer. This silver stand fits seamlessly under a classic white cake, enhancing its simple elegance.

though a cliché—is perhaps the perfect expression of your wedded bliss.

While some couples choose cake shapes that reflect an event or cherished memento—a famous monument where they were engaged, a beloved pet, an icon of their profession—the more conventional shapes and structures include: heart, rectangular, petal, hexagonal, round, square, sheet, separated tiers, stacked tiers, and satellite cakes. Discuss the style and setting of your wedding with your cake designer and ask him or her which shape will best convey the mood you're trying to achieve. Then ask to see photographs of the cakes he or she thinks would fit well in your setting.

How Much Cake Do I Need?

Every baker has a different idea of how many servings they can cut from a cake. The numbers vary slightly from baker to baker, due to each one's flavor options, so it's important to ask how many guests each tier will serve. For example, a dense, dark chocolate, nut, or fruitcake would generally be cut into smaller slices than a light, airy yellow sponge cake filled with butter cream or fresh fruit. Generally speaking, wedding cake slices, for a 3- to 4-inch-high cake tier, are approximately ¾ inches wide by 2 to 2½ inches deep. Also, square tiers provide more servings than round/petal/hexagonal tiers. Three tiers will serve 50 to 100 guests; you'll likely need five layers for 200 guests or more.

Some cake designers will suggest a cake size that will serve all of your guests in addition to a small tier that is traditionally saved for your first anniversary (see page 103). Don't be tempted to underestimate the number of slices of cake you will need. Internationally renowned cake designer Ron Ben-Israel warns, "I once had a client tell me that there were 100 fewer people on her guest list than she had invited. Someone had suggested to her that trimming the size of the cake was a good way to save money. As a result, the servings of cake were very small, embarrassing the caterer and more importantly, the bridal couple."

Opposite: A square cake is modern and fun; especially when several tiers are stacked like presents one upon the other. The sea-inspired decorations here, especially the kissing sea horses, echo the lighthearted mood of this cake, and couple.

Cakes and Weather

In general, warm weather presents the most risks for wedding cakes. Whether iced with fondant, butter cream or meringue, a wedding cake should never be placed in direct sunlight. Fresh flowers will wilt, decorations may slide, and worse, butter-cream cakes and chocolate decorations are at great risk of melting. Some decorations, such as pulled/blown sugar, crystallized flowers, and some gum-pasted decorations, can start to melt or look "tired" on very humid days. What's more, they are at risk of melting if they are stored in a refrigerator, as that too is a humid environment. A seasoned baker can tell you what ingredients, materials, and decorations are weather resistant in the venue you've chosen and how to keep the cake safe until you're ready to cut it.

Don't be tempted to underestimate the number of slices of cake you will need.

Once you have decided on the baker who's right for you, it's time to ask some essential questions.

How much do you charge per serving for the basic cake offered?

Do you deliver and set up the cake?

Is there a cost for this?

How will the cake be delivered?

Who will cut the cake?

Who is responsible for returning the cake stands and any other related items owned by the baker?

Do you have other cakes to deliver on the same day of my wedding?

Can you give me two or three references?

Then call every reference on the list before you make your commitment.

Opposite: Serving each wedding guest a single petit four is a charming alternative to a slice of cake. For a small, supremely elegant gathering, place each one under glass and garnish with fresh flowers.

CAKE TALK—A GLOSSARY OF TERMS

You don't need to have a professional's knowledge of baking in order to envision your dream wedding cake, but it may give you confidence to know some of the basic terms associated with cakes and, more specifically, wedding cakes, when you meet your baker.

Basket weave—A piping technique that echoes the interwoven reeds of a wicker basket, best achieved using butter cream and royal icing.

Butter cream—A light, creamy frosting made with butter, confectioners' sugar, egg yolks, and milk or light cream that stays smooth and soft and can be colored and flavored easily. It is used to render lifelike flowers, swags, and any decoration that can be piped. Butter cream can also be spread spotlessly smooth to create a perfectly flat surface on which to arrange decorations.

Cake tower—A multilevel, multiarmed cake stand used to display individual cake layers that surround the main cake.

Columns—Also known as pillars, columns are de rigueur in most traditional tiered wedding cakes. Tubes are placed between each tier to achieve open air between each of them. Unlike separators, columns are clearly visible and are part of the overall design of the decorated cake.

Cornelli—An intricate piping technique that yields a lovely lacelike design.

Dacquoise—A circular dessert consisting of layers of meringue mixed with ground toasted nuts and layers of whipped cream mixed with soft fruits.

Dotted Swiss—A piping technique in which tiny raised dots are arranged in patterns on the cake to resemble dotted-Swiss fabric.

Piping

Basket weave

Dragées—Sugar-coated almonds that come in a variety of sizes and colors, including silver and gold. They are used primarily for decorative purposes.

Filling—A fruit- or cream-based "paste" spread between layers within tiers of a wedding cake.

Fondant—A sweet, elastic confection used for both candy and icing, it is made of sugar-water and cream of tartar cooked to the soft-ball stage. It is extremely pliable and is literally rolled out with a rolling pin and draped over a cake. Fondant is excellent for achieving precise, architectural designs and decorative details.

Ganache—A classic chocolate and cream mixture that bakers use for many chocolate applications, from fillings and glazes to truffles. It has a very shiny, smooth finish.

Genoise—A classic European sponge cake. It is a tender but dry cake that is usually moistened with a flavored sugar syrup.

Groom's Cake—An old custom that is still observed at some weddings, a groom's cake is a separate cake, traditionally fruit-cake but more increasingly chocolate cake. It is usually served along with the wedding cake and cut into slices and packaged for guests to take upon leaving the reception.

Gum paste—This mixture of sugar, cornstarch, and gelatin can be molded like clay and turns hard and brittle as it dries. It is used to mold realistic-looking fruits and flowers to decorate a cake. While not as flavorful as marzipan, gum-paste decorations are edible and can be stored for years as keepsakes.

Latticework—A piping detail that consists of crossed strips arranged in a diagonal pattern of open spaces.

Columns

Groom's Cake

Marzipan—A sweet, pliable paste made of ground almonds, sugar, and sometimes, unbeaten egg whites that is used to mold edible flowers or fruit to decorate the cake. It can be tinted and molded into almost any shape and can also be rolled in sheets, like fondant, and used as icing.

Meringue—A mixture of egg whites, sugar, and air that is whisked and dried in a slow oven. Meringue can be shaped before drying.

Piping—Decorative details, such as borders, basket-weave patterns, and flowers, created by forcing frosting through a pastry bag equipped with various metal design tips.

Pulled sugar—A technique in which boiled sugar is manipulated and pulled to produce flowers and bows.

Royal icing—Made of egg whites and confectioners' sugar, this icing starts life as a soft paste piped from a pastry bag to create latticework, beading, bows, and flowers. When dry, its texture is hard and brittle. Do not refrigerate.

Sugar dough—A mixture of confectioners' sugar, water, cream of tartar, and tragacanth gum that can be molded like clay and turns hard and brittle as it dries. Often used for cake decorations. It is also known as *candy dough* or *gum paste*.

Torte—A dense cake that does not use leavening agents like baking powder or baking soda.

Whipped cream—Heavy cream beaten until soft and foamy. It is unstable and not recommended for outdoor weddings.

Cake tower

Marzipan

Royal icing

CHAPTER 4

Flavors and Frills

Remember how many wedding-dress styles you looked at before you chose the one that seemed like it was made just for you? When you first put it on, it made you glow on the inside and the outside? Your wedding cake should have the same impact; it should be as deliciously memorable on the inside as it is stunningly beautiful on the outside. The only rules that should influence your decision are that your cake must taste delicious and that it be big enough for everyone to enjoy a piece.

Flavor is as important as all the visual elements of your wedding; it makes an indelible imprint on memory. However, it needn't be overwhelming. A plain cake that tastes wonderful will be as well remembered as a visual stunner elaborately embroidered with pulled-sugar flowers. Flavors have personalities, too, so try to use the ones that reflect the mood of your wedding: Chocolate is decadent; vanilla, luscious and pure; spices, autumnal; lemon, sprightly and tart.

What's inappropriate? A wedding cake can be any flavor you want it to be, as long as the cake itself, the filling, and the icing are harmonious. "The ultimate test is if the cake simply doesn't taste good," says baker Wendy Kromer. "That, and if it doesn't stand up to being stacked or decorated as you'd like." She suggests that white or yellow cake can be combined with just about any filling and icing, while chocolate cake is best with chocolate, praline, mocha, or vanilla butter creams; chocolate ganache; and raspberry, strawberry, or orange fillings.

Nut-based cakes are well suited to fruity fillings and creamy icings. Christine Deonis, a New England cake baker, says chocolate cake with mocha filling and mocha butter cream icing is very delicious, while lemon pound cake with any kind of berry filling is equally successful. She advises against ice cream cakes and combining chocolate cake and lemon filling.

Special Touches

Cakes can also be decorated to provide a clue as to the flavor on the inside. For example, gum-paste orange blossoms can adorn a cake of orange chiffon layers spread with citrus curd. If you've decided on a cake covered with white chocolate ganache with fresh strawberry puree between the layers, you can provide a clue as to the flavors on the inside by artfully arranging marzipan wild strawberries round the tiers. If apricot jam separates the layers of your cake, why not surround your cake with the delicately colored fresh fruit.

Page 60: Flowers made from piped frosting can be as beautiful as the real thing. Roses in various stages of glorious unfolding add an exquisite flourish to this tiered white cake.

Above and opposite: If the fresh version of your favorite flower is out of season or isn't safe to place on the cake, you can still have it made out of butter cream, a very versatile medium for rendering almost any decoration imaginable, in any color. Here purple and white frosting lilacs are piped onto a charming chocolate layer cake.

SENSATIONAL FLAVOR COMBINATIONS

lemon pound cake with lemon mousse filling and vanilla butter cream

chocolate layer cake with chocolate filling and white chocolate fondant icing

applesauce or spice cake with cream cheese filling, dusted with confectioners' sugar

almond genoise and dacquoise layer cake filled with butter cream and iced with Swiss meringue butter cream

maple layer cake with maple butter cream filling and icing

carrot cake with butter cream filling and icing

coconut cake with lemon curd or strawberry puree filling and seven-minute frosting

lemon poppy seed cake with fresh lemon curd and lemon mousse topping

red velvet cake with white-chocolate cream cheese filling and frosting

croquembouche: cream puffs filled with pastry cream, stacked into a triangular tower, and bound in a web of whisper-thin strands of lightly caramelized sugar

cheesecake covered in fondant, butter cream, or marzipan

The trick to choosing just the right additional decorations is to express the style you've envisioned for this sweet celebration. Among the most popular flourishes are gum-paste or marzipan fruit and flowers. Piped butter-cream decorations are also frequently chosen by bridal couples, either for making handsome or playful borders around the tiers, for creating an overall pattern on all of the tiers, or for rendering their favorite flowers, birds, pets, or china patterns on their wedding cake.

Sugared fruits such as kumquats, crab apples, seckel pears, champagne grapes, and strawberries; leaves, herbs, and edible flowers glisten when gently arranged on a wedding cake. Dragées and gold leaf, too, can add the sparkle of silver and gold for a dramatic effect. Royal icing is an excellent medium for making delicate, long-lasting decorations; it can be used both to make fanciful patterns and to attach them to the cake, as it dries very hard. Of course, seasonal fresh fruit, flowers, and nuts will never go out of style, especially if they are artfully set atop the cake.

Opposite: Wild strawberries, fashioned from tinted marzipan, sprout from the tiers of a fondant-covered cake—an elegant contrast to stark white. The tiny berries also offer a visual hint that the filling is strawberry flavored.

Page 66: Sugared seckel pears and plums are arranged as if in a still life painting. On a smooth canvas of fondant they exude a simple elegance.

Topping It Off

The top of the cake is usually reserved for the pièce de résistance: a traditional ceramic bride and groom figurine, fresh or faux flowers or fruit, an elaborately tied marzipan bow, or grandmother's vintage cake topper. The options for cake toppers are unlimited, but the reigning favorite is fresh flowers. Some bridal couples prefer a bare cake top, especially if their cakes are minimalist and sleek. If you are set on a bride-and-groom figurine but can't find just the right one, your cake designer may offer to render one out of marzipan or may be able to lead you to someone who can.

"My favorite cake topper is 'something borrowed'," says cake designer Ron Ben-Israel, "like an antique bride-and-groom figurine that has been passed down through the family." Ben-Israel also suggests opting for something made out of sugar—swans, a castle, a keepsake ornament, and even a tiara. A rather handsome—and poignant—way to crown a wedding cake is with the initial of your new last name, made from fresh herbs wrapped along a wire letter or piped in royal icing. Some of the most poignant cake toppers are not brand new but old. Scour your mother's and grandmother's attic or china cabinet for a charming and suitable family heirloom. "Something old" is never inappropriate on your wedding day.

Page 67: *Some brides think baroque is best and can have it tastefully translated onto their wedding cakes. Buttercream flourishes and a looping crown look smart set atop this slick white cake. Sugared grapes with their leaves intact provide a lush base and topper.*

Opposite: *A frisky bouquet of tiny white blooms makes a lovely finishing touch to a square cake. The openwork basket-weave frosting recalls a garden trellis.*

Left: *Cake toppers can be almost anything, but the classic porcelain bride and groom will never go out of style.*

Page 70: *An heirloom bride and groom stand tall beneath a trellis of stephanotis on a towering four-tiered confection.*

What It Will Cost

The most successfully planned weddings begin with a well-laid-out budget with the cost of the cake claiming from 3 to 5 percent of the total amount you plan to spend on your celebration. This is the average amount, though some couples choose to trim costs in other areas in order to boost their cake budget. In most cases, the cost can be determined as soon as you decide how many guests will be attending and what kind of cake you want; cake designers price their cakes by the slice, and the costs range widely depending on where you live and what kind of cake you desire. In urban areas such as Atlanta, New York, and San Francisco, the base price may begin at $3 per slice or even more if you use a highly sought-after cake designer. The rates can range from $1.50/slice for a basic white or yellow cake with butter-cream frosting to $15.00/slice for a dense chocolate and nut cake covered in fondant with marzipan decorations.

Keep in mind that your choice of cake and frosting flavors will have comparatively less impact on price, as baking ingredients are relatively inexpensive. What really drives up costs are any handmade decorations, intricately molded shapes, and precise decorative details that require long hours to create. When you discuss prices with the cake designer, inquire about delivery and accessory rentals and whether you will be charged extra for the top tier—the one traditionally saved for the first anniversary (see page 103). Be aware that many cake designers require a 25 to 50 percent deposit.

Page 71: Butter-cream vines grow up from the base of a tiered cake, leading the eye to a porcelain bride gracefully dressed with a veil of real lace.

Above: A wedding in the woods inspired this multitiered basket-weave cake. The unusual—and humorous—brown bear topper is perfectly suited to the setting.

While your budget may dictate a simple cake, unceremoniously iced, there are many clever ways to trim the cost of your fantasy confection. With a little ingenuity and knowledge gained before visiting your cake baker, chances are good you can keep expenses down and still have the perfect cake on your wedding day. Consider using the staff pastry chef of the hotel, country club or catering service you have chosen rather than hiring a cake designer; you'll avoid cake-cutting fees, additional tips, and delivery costs.

Choosing fresh flowers for decorations and selecting butter cream for your icing are among the most frequently recommended cost-cutting tips. Forget about feeling that you're compromising: butter cream is delicious and nothing brings a cake to life more than fresh blooms. If you can't imagine forgoing your fantasy cake but can't possibly afford the high per-slice cost, ask your cake designer to make a small version for display and the ceremonial cake cutting then have him or her make back-up sheet cakes for serving guests. If the reception space requires a towering cake in order to stand out, discuss having a cake arranged satellite style with your baker. A satellite cake gives the illusion of height and breadth with a top layer of separate cakes tiered on top of a lower layer of separate cakes. Square tiers generally provide more servings than round tiers, though they can be more time consuming to construct and frost.

> **CAKE WISE**
>
> "I urge people to be very direct. If there is a budget issue, be up-front about it. You can't stretch something that isn't there. Let's say you can't afford a cake designer. Bringing a picture from a magazine to your local bakery and asking them to re-create it from the photo is not very realistic. Look at the cakes they've done successfully. Simplify. Keep it elegant and fun rather than creating a disaster."
> —Ron Ben-Israel, cake designer, New York City

If money is no object and you've allotted a larger-than-average portion of your budget to the cake, then let your imagination run wild. Molded flowers and fondant icings are among the most expensive choices, with the lifelike flowers driving the

price per slice as high as $5 to $10. Royal-icing flowers fall somewhere between fresh and molded, resulting in a $3 to $4.25 slice of cake. Depending on the flavors you choose, requesting a variety of cake flavors—a different one for each tier, for example—will increase the cost of your cake. If a multitiered square cake is your idea of the perfect wedding confection, expect to pay more for the labor involved in getting those tiers to line up perfectly and the icing to turn the corners without flaw.

Before you depart from your meeting with your cake designer, review each point in the contract. Don't be afraid to ask for specifics, including details as to which display items or cake accessories must be returned and what the charges are for failure to do so. Together you should create a precise description of the cake you've agreed upon and include that description in the contract. For example, clarify what "a three-tiered, fondant-covered cake decorated with gum-paste flowers" really means. Gum-paste flowers covering every tier? Cascading in a spiral from top to bottom? Or just ten scattered about? Ask your cake baker to discuss the ingredients he or she uses; whipped cream and Cool Whip are toppings with very different tastes. Don't hesitate to get the specifics; your baker will appreciate the clarity and so will you.

Choosing fresh flowers for decorations and selecting butter cream for your icing are among the most frequently recommended cost-cutting tips.

THE BAKER'S CONTRACT

As with all of the vendors who will supply professional services for your wedding, your baker should provide you with a contract for services you have both agreed upon. The contract should contain the following points:

Date of contract

Name and contact information, including cell phone numbers for the vendor and you

Wedding date, time, and location (be specific)

Detailed description of the cake (design, flavor, fillings, icing type, decorations, number of tiers, shape, topper, number of slices)

A list of items you're renting (plastic tiers, cake stand, columns) and how they should be handled after the wedding

If anything inedible (fresh flowers or greenery, gum-paste flowers that may have wires in them, plastic hardware) is used on the cake, it should be VERY CLEARLY stated in the contract and provisions made for what should be done with those items before serving the cake.

Delivery and setup fees

If the baker is responsible for decorating the cake table, a description of the decorations and the additional fees charged.

Total price

Deposit amount

Balance and due date

Cancellation and refund policy

Cake designer's signature

Your signature

Opposite: *Eye-popping displays of five "satellite" cakes surround a slender cake tower. Dowels divide the cake tiers, making room for luxurious bunches of roses and stephanotis. The monochromatic scheme is interrupted by only one color: the green leaves, which "loosen" the look just perfectly.*

CHAPTER 5

Cake Presentation

From Fun to Fabulous

At the ceremony, it is the bride who is the focal point, her beaming face and graceful stance accentuated by her dress, veil, flowers, shoes, and jewelry. At the reception, the main object of the guests' visual attention is the cake, and its structure and decorations should be enhanced by a distinctive presentation. Once you've determined what your cake will look and taste like, it is equally important to discuss with your baker how it will be presented. The possibilities range from the traditional—an elaborately decorated round cake table—or the unconventional—a stone birdbath for a garden wedding.

One couple who was married in an art gallery set their square, three-tiered cake on a pedestal, as if it was a sculpture on exhibit. Another couple celebrated their union in a big barn in Connecticut in which the cake was set upon towering bales of hay! The wedding cake can also be the centerpiece of a dessert buffet, stylishly arranged in the center of the table, surrounded by bowls and platters of varying heights (none ever higher than the cake) filled with candies and confections. If your style is playful yet elegant, you might set multiple cakes atop the arms of an appropriately sized plant stand.

Not all cakes need elaborate presentations or luxuriously dressed tables. A multi-tiered chocolate cake—a version of the layer cake your grandmother used to make frosted with broad strokes of butter cream—calls for nothing more than an equally charming painted bistro table with a "distressed" finish. One of the simplest ways to dress a cake table is to casually scatter the same kind of flowers that appear on the cake around its base. This is most successful if the flowers are long lasting. Alternatively, arrange tiny vases filled with flowers around the base of the cake for a simple decorative touch.

Take your presentation cues from the cake shape, color, and decorations. It should complement the design, stature, and style of the cake. For example, if a favorite childhood quilt inspired the piped decorations on your cake, clothe the table with fabric-similar in design and texture-or in the very quilt itself. If you are serving a traditional white cake, you can't go wrong with a pristine white tablecloth. Another option is to incorporate the colors of the bridal flowers or bridal-party dresses into the table decoration.

For some couples, the cake is as important as every other element of the wedding. If it is to you, as it was to one Connecticut couple, then by all means draw extra attention to it. One half of this bridal couple was an architect who designed and built a separate tent for the cake. He wanted to be sure

Page 76: A beribboned cake stars at a reception in the living room. Dessert dishes, teacups, champagne glasses and petit fours seem casually strewn on the round table, but they are in fact artfully arranged to frame the stunning cake.

Opposite: Cake and champagne follow a casual evening ceremony at home. A playful polka-dot cake, rimmed in bright green butter-cream leaves and set on a milk-glass cake stand, is long on charm and informality.

Page 80: Perhaps the simplest way to decorate the table on which the cake is presented is with heaps of fresh blossoms. Just be sure they don't touch the cake if they're not edible.

CAKE WISE

Ron Ben-Israel is not a fan of elaborately decorated cake tables. He believes the cake should really be the focus. If the cake is grand in and of itself, then there's no need for embellishment. When he is considering how to present the cake, Ben-Israel follows the example of great couturiers. "When clothes are made from the best fabrics and are cut to perfection, there is almost no need for accessories," he says. "If a cake is made from the best ingredients, has structural integrity and wonderful decoration, then that's enough."

all of the guests saw the cake and so designed the tent in such a way that the guests had to walk around the cake in order to enter the reception.

Beware the precarious presentation of the cake, however. Ron Ben-Israel recalls the wedding reception that took place in a large home with a sprawling staircase. The bridal couple asked that the cake be set on a table on the landing so that guests could see it as they walked in. The bride's young nephew was so taken with the sight of the cake on entering the party that he ran up to it and hugged it, leaving his face imprinted on the tiers. The good-natured bride was charmed, and the cake was served with laughter all around.

Cutting the Cake

Centuries before there were elaborately decorated, tiered cakes and ribbon-wrapped silver cake knives for slicing, the wedding "cake" was represented by barley bread, a symbol of the bride's fertility. The groom would eat a piece of the bread and break the remainder of the loaf over the bride's head, symbolizing the taking of her virginity and his dominance over her. Today, the tradition of "breaking bread" together has evolved as much as the original wedding "cakes" have. While today's cakes are still made of flour, a form of wheat, wedding cakes

can still be considered a symbol of the bride's fertility—or of a new life. But participating together in the ritual of cutting the cake represents a couple's commitment to share life's tasks and whatever paths their life takes.

Depending on the style of your wedding, cutting the cake can be reserved for the end of the reception or just before dessert is served. At a sit-down dinner or luncheon wedding, the cake is usually served immediately after dinner. At a buffet dinner, it is traditionally cut and served just before the reception ends. For a traditional cake-cutting ceremony, the groom puts his right hand over the bride's right hand and together they cut the first slice from the bottom tier of the cake. Sometimes they cut two slices, in order to feed each other a small bite. The cake is typically removed to the kitchen, where it is sliced and served to guests.

As wildly varied as wedding cakes can be, the ritual of cutting them has remained as tradition bound as the exchange of wedding bands. While some bridal couples today choose not to participate in the cake-cutting ceremony, the majority of brides and grooms find it as poignant as the exchange of vows. In this, your first shared task as a married couple, make a few special arrangements in advance to ensure that the ceremony is as joyous as possible. Designate a family member, or rely on your wedding planner if you are using one, to ask the bandleader or emcee to make a gentle announcement at an agreed upon time for the cake cutting ritual. If you have arranged for the cake cutting to take place with dancing and socializing time to spare after-ward, remind that same family member to tell the band to begin playing right after you feed each other a bite of cake.

According to tradition the cake should be cut just before dessert at a lunch or dinner reception and shortly after guests arrive for a tea or cocktail reception. A ribbon-tied silver knife is the traditional utensil to use. (This is never used to cut slices for guests: it's too thick to make precise cuts.) If you registered for a silver cake knife and have already received it, by all means use it. You may even want to have your

Opposite: A veritable rose garden surrounds a wedding cake displayed at an outdoor reception. The cake table should always be set out of the way of heavily trafficked areas—and safe from curious pets and little ones.

The custom of wearing a bridal veil is thought to be a vestige of the ancient bridesmaid's ritual of draping a cloth on the bride's head before the bread was broken over it.

initials engraved on it before your wedding day. An heirloom, such as the knife your parents used on their wedding day, is also a lovely choice.

Once the announcement has been made the bride and groom should stand just to the side of the cake. The groom should place his right hand over the bride's, and together they should cut into the bottom layer. Traditionally, the bride and groom feed each other a taste of the first slice as a symbol of their willingness to share a household. Some couples today have dispensed with this part of the ritual, while others find it poignant and symbolic. However you decide to share your cake with each other, it is never appropriate to stuff each other's mouths with cake. Once the cake is cut and shared between the bridal couple, it is removed to the kitchen where it is cut and served to guests.

Songs for Cutting the Cake

There isn't a bride and groom in the world who wouldn't love the chance to have two, three, or even four first dances as a married couple. Perhaps it is the very public performance of a very personal sentiment that makes it so exhilarating. A music-filled wedding can have a powerful impact on you and your guests, providing memories that will be remembered long after the last bit of cake is eaten. Why not choose a favorite song for the band or disc jockey to play when you cut the cake?

This ritual, too, is a public affirmation of your commitment to each other, and a favorite song can only add to the poignancy of the moment. Unlike the song you chose for the first dance, this song needn't be one you can comfortably dance to! Review the list of songs you considered for your first dance and reconsider those you thought inappropriate for the waltz or boogie. Chances are, there is a perfect accompaniment to the cake-cutting ceremony. Dinner music is also appropriate when cutting the cake.

Opposite: Cutting the cake is as much a part of the wedding ritual as the cake itself. The bride and groom hold the handle of the knife together, symbolizing their first shared sustenance of married life.

CAKE PRESENTATION

How to Cut a Tiered Cake

Most caterers have cut dozens of wedding cakes of all shapes and styles. Chances are they will not need any instruction on cake cutting. On the other hand, if friends or family are throwing your party, a bit of guidance may be needed in order to get the right number of slices from the cake. Be sure to have an apron, a thin, long knife, a spatula or cake server, and, if the icing is Crisco based, a warm wet towel to clean the knife between cuts. A stack of plates and enough forks and napkins for every guest should be close by.

The first step in serving the cake is to remove the top tier and the armature used to hold it up. This tier is traditionally saved for the couple's first anniversary (see page 103). If there is no anniversary tier, remove the top tier and set it aside, followed by each remaining tier. If your cake topper is an heirloom or has sentimental value and can be preserved, be sure to instruct your caterer to give the topper to one of your attendants for safekeeping. Begin cutting slices from the bottom tier. For a 16-inch round tier, make an impression of a circle about 4 inches from the rim of the tier using the sharp knife. Cut through the impression. Beginning with the outer circle, cut ¾-inch-thick wedges from the outer rim; you should have about twenty-four slices of cake. As you cut, hold the knife in one hand and a cake server in the other. Allow the slice to fall onto the cake server, then slide the slice onto the cake plate. Cut the remaining ring of the tier into twelve slices, each about ¾ inch wide. Continue cutting the smaller tiers in this manner, until you reach the smallest tiers, which can be cut like a regular layer cake. If the bottom tier is larger than 16 inches, make a second circle within the first and proceed as described above.

How to Serve the Cake

Custom dictates that it is bad luck for a guest to leave the reception without tasting the wedding cake. To preserve all of the good fortune that a wedding day promises

Opposite: *A long thin knife is best for cutting the cake. You will also need a cake server to catch the slices and slide them onto plates.*

(and to guarantee that nobody misses out on every element of your delicious cake), follow a few simple guidelines for serving the cake. For a sit-down luncheon or dinner, the bride and the groom and the bridal party are served first. The guests seated at tables closest to the bridal party table are then served, followed by the remaining tables, with the servers working their way out to the tables on the edge of the room.

If your cake is covered in edible molded decorations, is served with a sauce, or is accompanied by ice cream, be sure to review this with the caterer or family. Are there enough marzipan flowers to place two on each slice of cake? How big should the scoops of ice cream be? A dry run is a good idea: You can use a stand-in cake and decorations to determine these details in advance.

For a buffet-style reception, there are several ways to serve the cake. Often the slices are set out on a large buffet table, and guests are invited to help themselves to cake once the bride, groom, and bridal party have sat down to eat theirs. Another option is to serve the slices as you would for a sit-down luncheon or dinner, progressing from the bridal table on to the guests' tables. This works especially well for an informal wedding, in which guests are encouraged to circulate freely from table to table and dance as they wish after dinner.

Above: Wedding cakes are generally sliced in wedges, with care taken to include part of the decoration on every plate.

Emergency fixes

Professional cake designers never have emergencies; it is their business to ensure that no matter the circumstances, your cake is perfectly presented at your wedding reception. They do take preventive measures, however, and always have an emergency repair kit on hand. Wendy Kromer feels the best way to ensure that her cakes arrive perfectly is to deliver them herself. She carries extra decorations, icing, a pastry bag and whatever piping tips have been used, a spatula, Swiss army knife, dowel cutter, towels, and aprons. She uses these tools to put the final touches on the cake, once it has been placed on the cake table. In addition to spatulas, cardboard, dowels, and extra decorations and icing, Christine Deonis brings a small knife with a pointed tip to remove any stray matter that may float onto the cake during delivery.

CAKE WISE

"My most spectacular emergency occurred in the early days of my career. I offered to make the cake for my friends' wedding in New Hampshire," recalls Wendy Kromer. "My plan was to make the cake in New York City, then drive it all the way to New Hampshire. I designed a tiered cake, each one separated by one inch of space. The cake was completely finished and well refrigerated, and quite pretty, I might add, when I put it in my rented car, a hatchback. I arrived four hours later at the B&B where I was staying with the bride, opened the hatchback to find the cake had warmed up and the dowels inside had loosened. The car had shifted slightly, of course, during the drive, causing the cake to collapse on itself! I cancelled my invitation to the rehearsal dinner that night "due to my desire to put the finishing touches on the cake." I was up until 4:30 A.M., salvaging what tiers/flowers I could and baking a few new tiers. I only brought one tip with me, as that was the only tip I used on the original cake. Thank goodness the couple running the B&B were sympathetic souls and gave me full run of their kitchen. The saving grace of the whole fiasco? When I saw my friend walk down the aisle in her reworked vintage wedding gown, I couldn't help but notice that the design I created on her cake with that one tip, matched the design of the lace in her gown perfectly."

If the homemade cake lovingly made by your aunt did not survive the trip from her house to the reception intact, consider setting up the cake table in such a way (a corner, alcove, or up against a wall) as to help camouflage the damage. Position the cake with the perfect side facing the guests and the damaged side toward the wall. If a cake becomes runny from sitting out too long before the cutting ceremony, remove

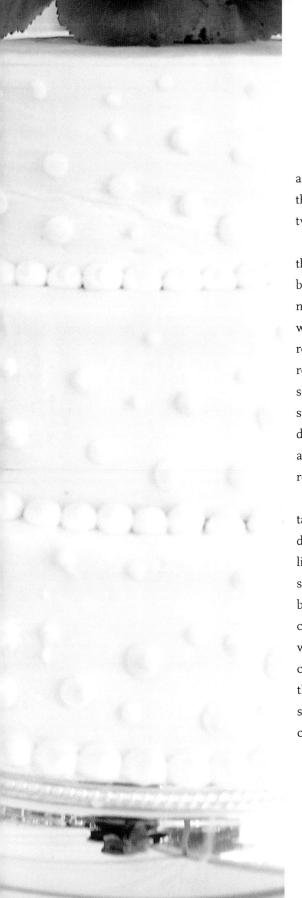

any perishable decorations and place only the runny tiers in the freezer for up to twenty minutes.

Preventing emergency fixes is far easier than patching up a cake that has slid off its base, or redecorating an entire cake that has melted before the reception. In general, the wedding cake should be delivered to the reception space just as it has come out of the refrigerator. An air-conditioned car will preserve the chill on the ride to the reception space. If the cake baker is traveling a great distance, it is wise to ice, decorate, and arrange the tiers at or in a space close to the reception (see Cake Wise, above).

Common sense dictates that the cake table be placed out of reach of wandering dogs and curious children, away from hot lights or large windows that throw direct sunlight. Appoint a friend or member of the bridal party to check on the cake periodically. Give him or her the authority to decide what actions should be taken if, in fact, the cake has sustained serious damage during the reception. If it begins to slide, fall, or seems to be in a precarious position, ask the caterer to remove it from the reception floor.

It is said that unmarried guests who place a piece of wedding cake under their pillow before sleeping will increase their prospects of finding a partner and bridesmaids who do likewise will dream of their future husbands.

Left: The wedding cake is always a great source of curiosity, and it is always charming to see a wide-eyed child stand before the cake. But a stray finger is less so. Put one of the brides-maids in charge of checking on the cake while it is displayed at the reception.

Photographing the Cake

Most wedding photographers will ask you for a
list of pictures that you want them to take on
your wedding day. From the scurrying of the
bride and her attendants getting dressed for the
ceremony to the fanfare surrounding the bridal
couple as they leave the reception, there are
iconic images of every wedding day that should
always be captured on film. Your wedding cake
is one of them.

CAKE WISE
Christine Deonis recalls
the one big scare she had
while delivering a cake.
"A car ran a stop sign and I
had to slam on my brakes.
The tiers shifted, but the cake
did not fall over, thank God.
Thanks to my emergency kit,
I was able to repair it to its
original beauty."

Laura Moss, a wedding photographer based
in New York City, says that she photographs the cake whenever she can. She arrives
at the reception space well before the ceremony begins, if the cake is scheduled to be
there. Moss suggests coordinating the timing of the cake photograph with the cake
designer or caterer. Much of the decision as to when she photographs the cake
depends on where the cake is placed. Sometimes it is set in a separate room, the easiest instance in which to get a great photograph.

She generally shoots many versions: the whole cake including the table, tight
shots of the whole cake and decorative details as well as shots of the couple cutting
the cake. If the cake is beautiful when sliced, she will take a picture of a plated piece.
"If the cake is in a setting that isn't particularly beautiful, I go in tight and try to cap-
ture just the cake itself in the photograph," says Moss. Natural light results in the
most beautiful images of wedding cakes; she suggests making considerations for the
photograph of the cake when determining where it will be presented. If the cake is
placed in a very dark space, she finds that candlelight placed around the cake results
in very beautiful pictures. "I never like to set up lights at a reception; they're unat-
tractive and are easily knocked over."

Opposite: *When photo-
graphing the cake, take a
variety of angles, including
distance shots as well as
close-ups. You don't want
to miss a setting as
beautiful as this one.*

CHAPTER 6

Grace Notes

At the reception, as in married life itself, it is the small, sweet gestures that make a difference. Among the easiest—and most charming—ways to create a unique and memorable wedding day is to present your guests with a tiny memento to take away. The custom of delighting guests with wedding favors, as they have come to be called, has its roots in Southern tradition, when the groom's cake, once exclusively a fruitcake, was sliced and placed in monogrammed boxes for each guest to take home.

It used to be that only unmarried girls received a piece, in order to place it under their pillows in hopes that the man they dreamed of would become their future husband. The groom's cake disappeared for several decades but is now making a strong comeback in flavors and styles as varied as the wedding cake itself. It is always smaller than the wedding cake—one or two tiers at most—but no less fanciful in its appearance. Chocolate cakes are very popular today, as are cakes rendered in the shapes of the groom's favorite hobbies or pastimes. The groom's cake is generally

Page 94: *Love is everywhere at a wedding—even in the confections. These heart-shaped cookies are whimsically decorated with royal icing and set in a dish, one for each table.*

Right: *For the groom who is a star grill master, why not a cake to call his own? A groom's cake can be as whimsical as the wedding cake; it is usually chocolate and somewhat smaller in scale.*

Opposite: *Modern grooms' cakes often reflect the passions of the husband-to-be. This playful rendering of jumping trout would make any avid fly fisherman's heart beat faster.*

Page 98: *When selecting the table sweets to enhance your cake, think about what to serve them in. This beautiful glass dish shows off the tiny frosted cookies to perfection.*

ordered from the wedding cake designer. They do not, however, provide the tiny boxes for transporting each slice. Be sure that you have provided these for the caterer to box the tiny slices.

Edible favors are always well received, and are not limited to tiny slices of the groom's cake. Anything sweet—candy coated almonds, iced cookies, tiny chocolates, petit fours—is appropriate. Packaged and presented in your own style, these traditional favors become unique to your wedding. Favors don't have to be limited to food; the only rules to remember are that they must be small enough to carry in your hand and be available in multiples.

As you've done for your flowers and food, take cues from the season for your favors. A small tree ornament is a sweet keepsake from a Christmas wedding, tiny gourds filled with flowers are lovely at an autumn wedding, and foil-covered chocolate turkeys are charming for a Thanksgiving wedding. A garden wedding might inspire tiny bouquets of just-picked flowers whereas a springtime celebration is the

perfect time to give your guests seedlings to plant in their own gardens and remember your special day. Perhaps the area in which you are being married lends itself to great favor ideas. A wedding in rural Vermont begs to showcase pretty bottles of maple syrup, whereas a ranch wedding in Texas brings red bandannas to mind.

The presentation of favors is another chance for you to put your personal stamp on your wedding day. Arrange them in a place that guests will be sure to pass by on their way out the door, or ask the caterer to set one on each place setting before guests arrive at the reception. Favors can also be passed. Give the job to the small flower girls and any young boys participating in the wedding. This bit of theater will charm guests, and the children will be happily occupied.

A word of advice on choosing your favors: The cost of a tiny memento may seem inconsequential to your wedding budget, but when you multiply it by 200 people, you can burst your budget fast. The costs include the favor itself, its packaging, and presentation. Many bridal

couples make their own favors or gather their friends in the months before the wedding to help them assemble their tiny gifts. If you are having difficulty finding a special item in bulk, look on the Internet; there are plenty of wedding websites with excellent sources for all manner of favors.

Cookies and Candy for the Table

A wedding cake is always awe-inspiring enough to stand on its own, but surround it with glistening dishes, bowls, and compotes full of variously shaped candies and confections, and its presence is majestic. Cookies and candy are never expected at a wedding reception, making them a cause for pure delight for guests young and old. No matter the sweets you choose, the key to presenting them beautifully without stealing the spotlight from the wedding cake itself is to place them in vessels of varying heights, none higher than the wedding cake. The cake should be placed in the center of the table, with the footed bowls, plates, and compotes surrounding it. The taller vessels in the back and on the ends; and middle-height and low dishes in front.

While there are no rules as to what confections to choose, following some general guidelines will guarantee a beautiful table. Choose sweets that are no bigger than one or two bites. Ideally, they will not clash, colorwise, with the wedding cake. For example, a traditional white wedding cake can be flanked by all-white sweets served in white dishes for stunning impact. Tiny white chocolates, dragées, white gumdrops, divinity fudge, coconut macaroons are all delicious white confections to consider.

Page 99: A romantic— and edible—lovebird rendered in meringue makes a wonderful dessert to serve at a small celebration. Meringues should always precede the serving of the cake.

Right: Cookie plates are often set on each table as the cake is being served. Ask your caterer to box those that have not been eaten to give to guests as they leave.

Opposite: For true lovers of sweets, a candy table is as important as a fabulous cake. Dragées, the symbol of fertility and the bittersweet nature of love and marriage, are set on a table alongside tea and champagne.

GRACE NOTES

On the other hand, pastel-colored candies set in silver dishes would beautifully complement a formal white cake. Many bridal couples want to have their favorite sweets at their wedding. The groom's favorite cookies, made in miniature, and the bride's favorite penny candy, can be cleverly presented in pretty stacks and in elegant footed bowls to give them wedding cake table cachet.

Savoring a Sweet Memory

Today, tiered cakes are sized to feed all of the guests at the wedding reception. But in the days when three tiers covered in white frosting was the only appropriate style, each tier assumed a specific role. The bottom tier was served to guests at the reception, the middle tier was sliced and packaged for guests to take home, and the top tier was reserved for celebrating the christening of the first child. While the reason for saving the top tier has changed, the practice has not. Today, it is often shared on the couple's first anniversary to celebrate the happy memories of the wedding day.

Many cake designers will include the top tier of the cake in the price of the cake; the remaining tiers are large enough to feed all of your guests so that you can save the top tier for your first anniversary. Ron Ben-Israel suggests the best way to preserve your cake is to refrigerate it until it hardens. Ask your baker which decorations can be saved. Sugar decorations can last for months and months, while marzipan, which contains almond oil, can be refrigerated up to three weeks. Wrap the tier in several layers of plastic wrap—do not skimp on the plastic—and freeze. The cake can be frozen up to a year and still taste good, says Ben-Israel, as long as it is made from pure butter. Any other fat used will break

While there are no general **rules** as to what **confections** to choose, following some **general guidelines** will guarantee a beautiful table.

Opposite: *Instead of giving a slice of cake to departing guests, consider petit fours made in the same flavor and frosting. The tiny jewel-like cakes will keep better than a slice because they haven't been cut.*

down slowly over the course of the year, imparting an "old" flavor to the cake.

The night before your anniversary, bring the cake gradually to room temperature by placing it in the refrigerator. Remove it from the refrigerator the next day, unwrap and bring to room temperature. Whether you've saved the tier of your actual wedding cake or re-created a tiny version on your anniversary, what better way to celebrate the sweet taste of love and marriage than with a symbolic slice of wedding cake.

Opposite: *A small sweet makes a wonderful parting gift for guests, especially when inscribed with a personal message.*

Photography Credits

PHOTOGRAPHY CREDITS

Index